Excellent Wildlife Photos

Clay Ventre

LILY POETRY REVIEW BOOKS

Dear Reader,

Here are some poems…Thanks for trying.

                    —C.V.
                       '25

"Thou hast seen nothing yet."

        —Miguel de Cervantes Saavedra, *Don Quixote*

Contents

FOREWORD

Clay Ventre's poems do what poetry allows poems and poems allow people to do. Take what's seen, heard, tasted, smelled and touched, into our brains, let it mix with all that is already inside: the language by which we learn to know our surroundings, the knowledge we gain because we listen and watch and wait for what living offers, and then, the inclination to see what all this might mean. This search for meaning, for a desire to understand that something is meaningful, that something has meaning, may be what allows us to believe life is worth living. Even when its meaning will not reveal itself except in glimpses, sideways, and as the quick-witted Emily Dickinson calls it, *slant*.

We experience glimmers of ever-lasting mystery via poetry in the case of Ventre's *Excellent Wildlife Photos,* written between 2012 to 2025, presumably to make something. This poetry, an old name for what is new every day, is not so much a category of linguistic organization but a way of understanding who we are and how we live. Garry Winogrand, who did not much photograph wildlife, remarks "There is nothing as mysterious as a fact clearly described. I photograph to see what the world looks like in a photograph."

I get a feeling as I read Ventre's poems that he writes poems to see what he's seen in the world in poetry. I get a strong inkling his purpose comes naturally out of his love of poetry, language, wit, characters, and what we're up to when we interact with one another, especially in romantic situations. His dialogues between an often and consistently invoked man and woman constitute some of the most delightful repartee in the book.

from The Aside

> Michelangelo got it wrong
> She said
> You should get it right—
> and while the rest of the
> party tried for conversation
> a thousand birds flew

between them
she carved him
into words
for future arguments
then
they rejoined
the party
him still at sea
she
a library on shore
all her books unread

These two likably lost souls engage in energetic raillery, riposte, crosstalk, quips, badinage, jocularity and persiflage, all in the name of maintaining a tension between them that could be called flirtation or seduction but those two words cannot cover the lengths Ventre is willing to go to give them room and time and words to accomplish their desire to be in one another's company.

Big things. Unmeasurable things. Uncontainable things. Unknowable things. Unifying things, ever mysterious, never to be pinned down. We can count on illusion to help us in our encounters with mystery. Mystery that can't be solved, mystery a perpetually persistent piece of who we are. We don't even know where we come from. We don't know where we're going.

How do we live with that? Occasionally we make up ways to confront it head on. Art. Religion, Philosophy. Sometimes we make up things to distract us. Art. Religion. Philosophy. Cervantes pushed Don Quixote to the brink over and over again. Sancho, poor Sancho, had to have so many near death experiences. I think of them when I'm reading Ventre. The quest to live a chivalrous life is everywhere present in Excellent Wildlife Photos. Its presence sometimes invoked by its absence, by behavior and attitudes, and words that seem the opposite of gallant, high-minded, lofty, magnanimous. In Ventre's book knight-errancy, in order to be honored, must be downplayed.

This too embraces a fine tradition. That of the Fool. The Trickster. Rule-breakers. and the kinder kind, Magicians and Wise Fools. Loki.

Puck. Pan. The Cheshire Cat. Coyote, Jack Straw, Sancho and Don Quixote, too. Maybe most of all, Hermes. Hermes, messenger of the gods, cunning, conniving, eloquent. Inventor of the lyre.

The song lyric writer holds the lyre's sound of music card to uplift their words, not unlike words in a poem and what they mean and where they've been and how they've been used are lifted by poetic traditions from all the long ago and far away unknown poet makers to the poet makers of today. The troubadour Tom Waits can say/sing these words: *the spotlight looks like a prison break* or *The seas are stormy, and you can't find no port. Gotta come on up to the house*...and the song's music will make Wait's words more than they are on this page.

Same with poetry, its music, in Ventre's case strongly influenced by line breaks, along with the natural sounds inherent in words and word combinations, work to transcend linguistic shenanigans, everyday cliché, and our eternally threatening inclinations toward self-pity, and melancholy. Poetry gives us a way around all this. It may even save us from ourselves. It may even give us a little respite while we wait for something or someone to change our minds.

from The Thing (is)

> You look like an oddly rendered
> Executioner
> She said
> Well there's a dark
> and inconceivable thing
> only a string quartet could get at
> He said
> We could hire one
> She said

Words appear to be stable when we see them on a sign, shirt, dish, canvas, wall, in the sky, page or screen. And yet, we know them to rise into our consciousness with the swiftest motion imaginable. In no time. Ventre finds words everywhere in every location, profound and profane. He takes his chances, going right up to and sometimes crossing the line between goofing and wit. The center of his vision of our lot in life is love. When love's the hub, how passionate can passion be, how profound, and when necessary, how self-deprecating, how ready for heart-break must one be? There can be no too much, too many, no overboard, no superlative superlative enough. Humor can be a talisman, an evil eye to keep disappointment at a distance. Sometimes it works. Is it true or even sometimes true that in order to make sense, everything has to be bigger or smaller than its usual self?

When one listens to the sounds of shoes on stage or the sounds of fingers on strings, those sounds may seem peripheral, or felt as a byproduct of the central activity producing them. Instead it turns out that those sounds are exactly the ones underlining the vitality of what we witness, the very real reality of the living arts. Ventre's tendency is to embrace broadly just about everything he encounters. Be it Mars, museum-going, music, painting, shoes, war, bones, or as in Penelope's case, making certain the everyday always comes with epic potential.

It's current to say, *put a pin in it,* when something rates saving. Maybe to spend a little more time with it, may be something we want to keep in our sights. Something we write down to remember it. Something, as it is being written, begins to be something else. It might become a poem.

Seeing the meticulous, delicate, precise ways butterfly collectors employ pins begins to turn somersaults of mobius gymnastics in my brain.

That which is the living embodiment of the beauty of live motion is stopped in its looping, swooping, gliding, glorious tracks, drugged to death, and displayed in all its deadly beauty by means of pins and glass and wooden structure, all manufactured, all made by the same makers who adore what their desire has destroyed. That is one kind of irony. An irony of human proportion, of human longing. What is it that makes us humans want to own what is ruined by our ownership? Irony and its equal, paradox, find themselves in many places in the circles we encounter in *Excellent Wildlife Photos.* One of the great things about these two, paradox and irony, is that they always speak for themselves.

from Strangle the Curator

the squirrels are in charge
the horses were just boring
after all
and the pastry boxes
were only fooling
and empty on opening
it's/ken'sep(t)SH(ew)el/
it's ok

Wallace Stevens for all his high church talk, gives us this as well: *Chieftain Iffucan of Azcan in caftan/Of tan with henna hackles, halt?* This is another kind of exaggeration. It's a paradox when a poem exaggerates. As it always does. This explains why larger than life alleviates obstacles to one's peaceful surrender to whatever it is whose inevitably isn't wanted. Ventre's poetry seems to know this, and believe this, even if by other means, on other terms.

from T-Minus

That space suit
makes you look old
She said
I'll make up for it in swagger
He said
You'll burn up on reentry
She said
I'm only going to the
supermarket
He said
Still...

Poetry is one of the desirable results of our brain's ability to never stop searching, shuffling, sensing, saving. Sometimes in an ecstatic state, as we experience a mind having a mind of its own. Sometimes we count on the ancient catalyst we call poetry to do a lot of its work on its own. We don't often find ourselves in the position of telling poetry what to do. Why would anyone want to tell poetry what to do?

We can't know beforehand what it might lead us to think. Poetry's thrilling ability to be flexible, divergent, layered, and exciting in ways one's own mind is not. Oh, each mind is flexible, divergent, layered and exciting for sure, though in its own ways and not in some other's mind's ways. We need to experience how one another thinks. Poetry is an extremely reliable route to other ways thoughts get thought.

When I'm in the midst of a poet lending their thoughts to mine, freeing me from myself, giving me alternative ways of thinking—as spending some days reading *Excellent Wildlife Photos,* which by the way there are none of in this book, provided, I'm grateful to poetry and to poets.

Each mind will house its own lexicon, its own music, its own way of linking things together. Fishermen, mechanics, farmers, cooks, nuns, brokers, prison guards, librarians, coaches, nurses, lawyers, fabricators, jewelers, farriers, real estate agents, spies, tree surgeons, weather forecasters, fletchers, each one of us knows some-thing about the world by means of the language we speak. Poetry protects all this knowledge.

Someone else's poems will be thrilling because they do not think the way one's own mind thinks. And that advantage goes without saying.

from This Tinier Opus

> no better beasts
> to marvel at
>   lovely meandering fools
>   longsuffering
>   godbeautiful
>
>
>   breaching for air
> over and over
> devouring
>   plate by plate
> a lifetime

Dara Barrois/Dixon

Excellent Wildlife Photos

Biography

¿Where have you been?
She asked him

He said
Twelve years ago I was standing next to a random dog outside a tobacco store.
A woman hands me an old flip phone, saying it's for me, then walks away.
I say hello into the phone and someone's yelling back in angry Russian
couplets. The phone went dead within seconds, there was no one to give it
back to, so I kept it. I never saw that dog again.

Alright
She said unfolding and

handing him an envelope
stamped

Your Life—Do Not Bend
he straightened up

on reading this
unwavering

resolute

This Book Changed My Life

after John Berryman

This cape fit
so I wore it
and fought crime

This box of candy
wanted a new home
so I stole it

This sky
looked lonely
so I threw it a bird

This typewriter
clacked too late into the movie
so I wrote a new ending

This dusty floor looked
just right so I became a priest
and blessed it

This name was left wandering
in ears so I changed it
to Alloisious

This book changed my
life into one filled with paprika
so I advanced upon it

despairingly

On the Menu in the Most Boring City in America

At the 53rd annual Alberto Giacometti
appreciation luncheon in Lubbock, Texas
the lunch fare included:
Chicken confit
Onion soup (French)
Bouillabaisse
Salmon en papillote
Quiche Lorraine
Croque monsieur
Boeuf bourguignon
Lamb shank navarin
and to satisfy the appetite of
the 103 year old Colonel Spencer—
King Ranch Chicken Casserole

The guest speaker for the day
came hobbling late to the event
complaining
that every time he walked
God
placed a stone in his left shoe

Alice Freebuckle—
aghast—
didn't believe him
The Lord would never stoop to
to that level of tomfoolery!
She huffed
I promise ma'am
Said the guest speaker
it is at least the case in my experience
that the Almighty—for what must be good reasons
we mortals—lacking the faculties of reason
necessary to decode the meaning

and wisdom of such—
most certainly does!
This exchange ended the meeting—
the members of the Societé for the Appreciation
of the Art and Genius of Alberto Giacometti
were all equally aghast now
(except the Colonel—whose chin was laying
on his white tunic like an innocent barber)

They
leaving all the food to the birds and beasts
—all revelations undiscovered
—rose up
and quit the field

Irascible Among the Daisies

Breakfast, Sunday Morning,
2036, Mars
Musk Estate

Awake by the collar
and dragging an unwilling
holographic dog
on an imaginary walk
to the place where
you'll trade the dog
for a tank of
oxygen for your
brittle lungs
so you can sing
without coughing-up
something like
a kindness
a memory
a smirk
a museum
for all the mistakes
that came with your
birth
undone after your
death
a sign over the door
—No Admittance—
in other words
everything is prodigal
with daisies and ice cream
for the pathologically unsure
served by the last woman
on earth
named Sandy

The Pact

Let's declare war
She said
And invade each other
¿What's the triggering event?
He asked—and so
they explored the landscape
of that question like
blind cartographers
with caresses
and kisses of obvious
distraction (she had no answer)

If war was to come
they agreed to write
letters home to each
other while away on
campaign against
each other—and that each
one read something like

"My Dearest _____,

   In the end, the worst injustice of this necessary war is that it
makes a foreign country of the place I gave my heart
so completely to."

but without a trigger
and only minor border
skirmishes over where
to eat out
their war never started
—never ended

and every night they
held each other under
the searchlights
of zeppelins overhead
—that soft—playful light
their only payload

Stradivarius

Was famous for falling
in love

For having an artificial grandmother
—because the original he never knew

He sent unopenable packages
to arborists and carpenters

He made unfulfillable appointments
with epic women

who promptly
unliked him

but he stayed (most famously) in Love
He found wood more promising than

television
Learned math as argument and

—anticipating Foucault
made a mess of mass and wine

he found a friend who also had
an artificial grandma

so they could put the two together
and watch the sparks fly

and the two new friends could listen
and cry
He got olde

and then older

then a bit younger

because fame found him

again from falling in Love (again)

—world famously

even Wisconsin found out
and celebrated

Everything Exits

Bows like
bending willows
a descending
glissando of leaving
universal
in all the ways
to be gone
axiomatic
like stone while
catastrophe maidens
unvoicing all our names
till history folds
and every dollar
is spent
and so like
spring
a quiet intermezzo
connects us in
a mini-series
of bad ideas
and cliché-peddlers
embarrassment-clowns
and staycation travel writers
before we can arrive
before we can meet for real
just in time
to miss that train
before we can embrace
we exit
we spill rain
like gods

Hard Knowledge

Grandpa—it turns out
played a glowing banjo
for the infamous
death-camp commandant
Singular Mingling
otherwise known as Nicotine Pete

Gramps played
and Pete would swoon
and swim
a fish in a jar
harmless at least

until grandpa's fingers
cramped and bled
and he had to stop

So he stopped—
what else could anyone do?

The Art of Thinking on
Earth at 3:13AM

It'll only bother you
if you think about it—
She had told him
when asked about the
dinner she would be
eating on Mars with
the previous owner
of her iron heart—
now—with her enjoying
0.375 gravity
and him without a
spaceship
he let his mind wander
a museum of possibilities
until he found himself
in its unlit cellar
—at night
with an unseen hand
guiding him in circles
like a clueless lion arcing
around a hunter who
at this distance
couldn't miss

Extended Angular Advice for
the Pathologically Unsure

If down
beyond repair

defunct

if a stuckboat
in a sea of molasses

all gestures
down and out

if a hammer
        is rusty

if a laughbox
        is broken

as downtrodden
as a misplaced
tube sock puppet

brass knuckles
gone all
flowery

motivation
long away
and over the hills

if as malfunctioning
as a loose cucumber

if the rain

has hit the dustbin

and sentiment sits off
the shoulders (oversized
flannel and
gray)

if found to be all silly putty
in the gnarled hands
of the unassailable
gods

then
pitch the baby
down the well

stop all payments
to the down and out

salt the land

sitgrumpy

spewbile

take all day to run
to the rescue

lay banana peels
in the path
of the already
square and tipsy

on a table
tapaway
a friend's
concentration

brickup
the butterfly

let nothing
rest

or

you could always nail
a fake Mondrian
to the side of your house

to ward off any marauding impressionists

their
fancy-pants jiu jitsu

dappled
in light and shadow

or maybe

just keep a horse in your head

one that
is relentlessly standing
and sad
in the rain

be still like that

there'll always be time later

to rescue a turtle
to a fanfare of bugles

to see you did good

and sleep like an idol
in the hands of
a believer

Storytime for a Dawn

If the aliens come back
it'll be to revisit that
molecularly delicate
dance
remembered
in an unsolicited
dream—one hand
in the air
one on a belly
hips swaying like
that heavenly pendulum
that marks the passing
passion of queens
for their kings—
their sad realm
an object of affection
to a tentacled thing
with a clipboard

Luv

That collection of
dumb shit
you thought you'd
never
(ever)
show anyone?
like the full set of
Scandinavian miniature
porcelain trumpet-playing
dancing cats? or
all those 1st pressing
ABBA albums?
of course you'll show her
all that—
you tripped
falling
your grip
on the edge of the world
is slipping
her hand is there
ready to save you
   she just wants
a sign
      something
breakable
adorable to a soundtrack played
through a diamond needle
that would still amaze any grandfather
to pieces

People Lay on Beaches Like Dried Flowers Waiting

1.
You can finally give that dog
a name
the one that followed you around
but never did bite you
like when someone
says —I know—
in that sad
shitty way
a whispering claxon
ruthless with dramatic
rhythm and claustrophobic
kindness between interruptions
of long wars of oil on canvas
no one reports on because
there's always something
tiny in petulance-sauce
staring up from the menu
poking a stick
at us while
all we're trying to do
is die as late as possible
and with as little trouble as possible
like a reverse birth
something beautiful maybe
a cesarean
a temporary wound
in the sky
custom-made for each of us
to unhinge into
everything we leave behind
an instant museum

2. (a city, early morning, late capitalism)
The One thought the Other
Was out there somewhere
Keys for hands
Always unlocking something
Head full of beginnings
Looking for endings
The One thought the Other
was out there somewhere
¡I exist!
The One would say
In a thick French accent
Atop a crumbling water tower
Atop a building nestled
In a radio play
Converted to an audiobook
Transcribed into a night sky
The Other could read
Like an astronomer
Or a Batman
And come shining
Like the Sun
Blasting the dazed escapees
Of a dark movie theater
Or the tiny shock of green
climbing
out of a sidewalk
Carrying the song
of the Other who
planted it there
The One might find the Other
Over that tiny green song
And forget how they arrived
The One on a unicycle
The Other on round-bottom shoes
This is the farthest thing

from a farm
The One would say
Indeed
Said the Other
Voiced tinged with incracktifytis
They were sitting at the corner of
Strange Yet Not So Much and 52nd
They shrugged with whys
¿What's with the silence?
The One said to the Other
The Other thought so long
about this
A generation of volunteers
for the experiment of love
Came and went
then came again

The Search for Empathy Shot on Eastman
Color Negatives using the Technicolor
Dye-transfer Process with a Halftone Gray
Print Superimposed to Create a Visual
Effect Reminiscent of Old Nautical Prints

¿Ya know how
when you just wanna
sink like a sick and
tired whale under
all the ships overrun
with tiny little sailors
who want to spear you
for your tophat and
buttons to spend
like olde fashioned
funnysounding money
on something grandma
would commemorate
in quilt form
repeatedly pricking
her finger until
all her blood ran out
and the weight of
water was not enough
to undo the day?

It's like that

Carving Up an Omelet in Salinas

to the strings of
Angelo Badalamenti
and waiting for any museum
to open
and a bus boy came up to my table
and said
¿My apologies
are you done with the plate?

Everyone here is sorry
for something
or begging my pardon
or excusing themselves
and the place is filling up
with regular eaters
from out of town
and they're just regular-nice
with pockets full of
handshakes waiting
to be thrust on the
unsuspecting

And I'm thinking of
the one-way streets
ending here
and now the waitress is back
asking me if there's anything else
anyone here can apologize for
I'm good
I said
¿What time does the museum open?
I asked
It'll never open for you

She said
So sorry
She said
¿Can I get you a check?
She asked
No
I said
You remind me of someone
and I don't think I deserve
to leave here until I figure out
who that is
I said
she hip-checked one
of the normal-nice people
approaching my table
with an extended hand
and said
The coffee's bottomless
and—
beg your pardon —
you're welcome to die here

From behind me
some other
better
version of myself
cleared his throat
with panache
and a ticket in a pocket

Admit One.

Shift
or
The Arrival of Good King Hairpiece

It's almost like
—without warning
something we were
warned about happening
happened
and all of a sudden
it was like dodging
squirrels on speed
the way they darted
like furry pointless
scholar-missiles
avoiding the obvious
to chase the just south
of credible
the west of normal
returning after all that
geometry
to lay their nuts
of crazy
at the altar of a shifting
god of perpetual
self-pity
spastic
rudderless
all at sea
contagious.

Bad in Italy

talling at the balcony

yelling

and
one after anothering
with crossed arms

and nodding a face
like a fist

—so boring

elsewhere,
a morning is on
and the coffee purrs

and cigarettes are svelte
and lovely
at lips

Found Umbrage
or
1/2-Time @ the Olympics of the Gods of Sarcasm

I heard Beatrice had quite a scare
with a blue-footed fascist tapir
Sandy said
with all the certainty
of a *New York Times* op-ed

but we all knew
this was silly fantasy

Tapirs don't have blue feet
Sandy
We said with clerical certainty
and castigating clarity

and we all circled around her
with a kind of eighteenth-century
awareness

we blew Jacobin sighs and
we brazened-up
with quiet calamity
everywhere Sandy was not
and all at once
turning
opprobrium-fingers
pointing

with tongues tortured dry
teeming with
tsk-tsks
now

finally
after all these minutes
we were perfect

Brutal Butter Petition

after Andrea Cohen

like
slovenly spoken air
as steady as
a slow drying tango
more now
than your demand
for more
butter
for the anyway uncertain
arrival of pancakes
ordered at the table
you gained without waiting
(therefore)
(and forever)

              you win

And Then You Went Walking

in search of some god
imp or demon
who would sell you the sky
that you could own it
that you could give it to her
that you could let a forearm
go numb and die
under her head as she gazed
at her new prize
wondering
how the hell you could afford it

Let's Hope the Machine that Kills Us is Elegant at Least

Run
save yourself
I'll hold them off with borrowed
and boundless charisma
Take all you can hold tight to your breast
and hide-out
til my breathing stops
I'd say sarcasm them to death after I'm gone but
the machine doesn't fall for that shit
At times you'll have to be a gun
At times you'll have to be pieces of gold
At any rate, you'll have to stop being the sun
But continue confusing them
Arrive Riding on your own name
on the back of some even-toed ungulate
There was a time before America came ambling
Go tell your uncle about it
You always got on with it as Hamlet never could
Sparing us the trembling mess

Genghis Khan's Footstool

¿What's that?
He asked pointing down
to a footrest-like thing that
was maybe goatskin
stretched over the bones
of the last guy
to ask that question

I got it a flea market for
the terminally optimistic
She said
he thought maybe she
went there by accident

¿Does it smell bad?
He asked
Very
She said
then he thought he should ask
more questions because
of her answer

that maybe they would
start a conversation
that would keep them
in the same room for
at least 7 minutes

but she was just passing
through
stepping like the floor
was covered in lizards
she'd rather not tread on
and on the way out

she pointed to a dusty
chess board
and said
Your move
and he thought

her voice sounded funny
with that clothespin
pinching her nose
then
it was just him and the lizards
again

and still he had no move for the
chess pieces
he went over to the footstool
bent low
and couldn't smell anything

How does the Rain

and who became
so important

you couldn't

e X h a l e

without considering
the effect of your
breath

on

her train
huffing

on the track

towards a night

where you're

not

and why the sudden

need

to notice
when she finds

your lack,

your empty
head filled with

your stupid
        enthusiasm
for dumb light and
ridiculous
sound

a poetry machine
is broken

for

good

this time

the birds are playing
chicken again

swooping

across the road
and in front

of your speeding

car

daring you to

The Bad Bard

writes about every vulgar bird
and their soulless nests

scribbling-desperate

like running for a bus, clutching
a bust of Louis Vuitton,
that was never going to stop
anyway

His Amateur Cardiologist
on Vacation

She's gone —
(we'll say away)
so he starts
a project of himself

placed like a jar of
thoughts in a clearing
walled-in by arborvitaes
where he could write
the book—Penelope,
an Appreciation—but sitting

with the preternatural
beating in his chest
she once noted
and claimed
for herself (a condition
he thought to name
after her)

he thinks to ask the birds for
a little quiet so he could
listen for the sinking of
the sun—if there was an
off switch for his
strange heart
he'd hit it now
—before the dark

A Couple of Sad
Undead Babylonians

After a sculpture by Stéphanie Williams

10,000 years of questions
grew limbs of ruin
between them
so they forgot the place
they conjured out of
baffling cuneiform
and crumbling ziggurats
sustained with tribute
and plunder—advanced
forward with radio-waves
from space
situated between rivers
of bragging and boasting
about how they eschewed
bragging and boasting
and that only the gods
could really understand
their suffering of questions
answered with more questions—
¿Why are you always
weighing things?
He asked her
¿Why do you wear an
eyepatch over
a perfectly good eye?
She answered
I don't know
He said squintingly and
peripherally surprised
watching her carefully
assessing the heft of memory

—music was pressed and
folded into remembering
and wine was for forgetting

Almost Paris in the Rain

I should warn you
She whispered in the dark
If I accidentally
mail you my scars
it's no sign of anything
other than the failure
of language to get
to the bottom of
anything
oh—
—and
don't go climaxing over
midday naps in
uncertain houses

outside the rain stopped

Later
alone in a vegan restaurant and
needing to be sure of something
he told the person taking his order
No kale

Absolutely
No kale

Anais Unpronounceable

while John
is agonal in love
and Kohichi balances
trouble and home
fixing home
only to die anyway
Monique cries
a constant piano of rain
(maybe we lay
 on the floor)
Grendel loves your
tact all sticky
with whatevers
then startled
to nervous little fishes
as Steven Unapproachable
otherwise known as
Mr. Forlorn
brings his 3-stage
rocket-powered *all that*
to the party
all this and God
who rattled
God's tongue
from some elderly distance
epic
and sheer rock-
faced

Like Harvard but in Tokyo
(or Budapest)

An incredulous librarian
stares from behind
a bulletproof
salad bar sneeze guard
still dreaming long books
of the Treaty of San Francisco
or The Life-Cycle of Moths
sees the black hole
of a waiting piano
thinks
there must be a cross-reference
for this
maybe involving a history of Versailles
or the biography of Houdini
—then
all the news is delivered
all at once and shimmering
and the librarian's hands
unfold like a flower
and make a museum
we enter
pay
and are exactly as amazed
as we should be

Must Cultivate Stern Mars-Face Look
Before Leaving for Mars

and we admit to some
Disneyland dilemma
and the queen of legit
cooks the king of yesterday's
surprises
with string theory
for the lord of slings and arrows
who eats all over
our best cultivated
space travel faces
and we don't make it off the rock
and brows go dismal
with shame
till we remember the machine guns
in our heads
and we skim like zirconia
with the satellites
over Ohio

Maybe Beluga Lugosi Then

In the cozy restaurant
of the ark and chill inside me
the cooks have matured and
found jobs as accountants
the waitstaff are afflicted with zealotry
the barricades are memories
destined for muddy ebullience like
history stuffed into a book
some kid will withdraw from
the elementary school library cuz the cover
was cOoL and forget to return—

I think I am less in pieces because of
the glue I may be to others—
(If so) and I'm pretty sure
someone brought me to the ocean
because they thought it was mine to reclaim—
Rachmaninoff is on the radio again
but this time it's all galloping
horses and something that passes for dance—
In some memories there is a circle of
something I'd give to a would-
be lover wrapped in something like rain
something no one could cut
w/o looking foolish as a Slapstick Hero
with an oversized pair of scissors or
as beautiful as a faithful friend

This morning the wind startled
the leaves off the trees like
a stupid dog scattering
a flock of pigeons
I drove by the billboard that asks

what would I name a beluga whale and
of course
Worcester would beg
my opinion on that
—being landlocked
after all

On the Shores of the Mediterranean

Here's your problem—
you like boats that wash up
on the shores of the Mediterranean
where there you might expect to find
your grandmother who you grew up calling
Nadda because you couldn't pronounce
Nonna and you learned too late after she died
for you to ask her how she survived the war
by selling dust to the sky while hidden
under the rubble of her favorite tobacco store
where the proprietor ate-up all the misery in town
and rented a boat and rowed far out
on the Mediterranean and spit it out so it mixed
with all the water of the Mediterranean
and the fish of the Mediterranean breathed it in
and were caught by the local fishermen who
brought it back to shores of the Mediterranean
—or would have
if not for the storm whipped-up by the local
priest who developed a grudge against God
and so took to casting spells on the waters
of the Mediterranean
so the boats washed up
on the shores of the Mediterranean

becoming the rib cages of dinosaurs you mistook

for just a plague of boats that washed up

on the shores of the Mediterranean

where you wanted to open an art gallery

the small kind you could show your Nadda

if she ever crawled out from under the past

and made from the bones of bored romantics

syphilitic show stoppers lazy

on the shores of the Mediterranean

who gave themselves to art so you could

live cheaply above your tiny gallery

in a crooked apartment of plaster

mixed with your pulverized breath

and painted brown

with no room inside to swing a baguette

but big enough to have those

tuberculosis parties with all your personally

hand-picked literati friends and wait out

the storm of a short life by monstering on stilts

or trolling under the history that you know

from books books books you can't return

to the library because the library is burning

adding smoke to the smoldering ruins

of a flayed woman forming something like

a new religion dousing a lighthouse with

emerging numbers to make math

on the shores of the Mediterranean

where you cast-off a house with someone

you love inside—floating alone while

the evolving ghost of you grows more separate

from everything so even a trembling palm

shuts tight before it would take your money

so it seems you made it to the moon after all

without any booster rockets

just a will to unhinge from one shore

                                    to another

The Mollusk in the Room

¿Do Mollusks Dream?
He asked her over breakfast
Your friend left his dying brother
for you to look after again
She answered
he's in a cardboard box in the shed
She said
he went outside
and when he came back in
his unfinished breakfast
was gone and he said
His brother is dead out there
Then you didn't do a very good job
She said
No argument from me
He said
they talked for hours over the sound
of birds about what art was and
what to do about it
about where to go see it
about all the different ways
to experience it
to make it
whether food or shoes counted as art
they started to feel pretentious
which silenced them deeper
into the couch they were sitting on
then the sun went down and the day
was spent
About the those Mollusks dreaming—
He said in the dark
They do
She said
He didn't think to ask about what

What's the Palate Cleanser
for the Greasy Food of Misery?

If you taste your
misery like you got hit
by a freight train of
recognition like
when you read about
Steinbeck's kid-character
Frankie dropping the tray
full of drinks at the party
and running away from
himself like a broken flock
of startled birds
then there is none—
the taste is yours forever
or at least until
your tongue goes numb
with age
and every meal is a host
of memory
green
like summer under your feet
when you could step
on anything
without thinking
of the risk

Dizzy in the Fog of Always Taking a Turn
for the Worse

I've found these lessons useful in that I
didn't follow them:

Avoid "projects"

Pay attention

I saw the Embarrassment Ahead
signposts every few miles
and didn't heed them

Avoid being obviously untruthful

(¿Who can truly say they like the sound
of a harpsichord
and mean it?)

Don't dilly-dally

(I hesitated epically at the root
of that house I wanted
to buy and burn down
and was outbid
by a teething dentist who
practiced aural-oral surgery
through whispering only)

Try resourcefulness

I can build loneliness out of whole cloth
—understand it to be a gift of shelter against
any comedian or unwanted guest

I can build loneliness out of whole cloth —wear it out
—and start again.

Meteorology

He made another
storm that broke
into a clear sky
without her
and staggered like
a spent Ulysses
a blinkered
stupefied animal
come home—
a Penelope behind
every fake door
and covered in birds
in an enormous room
where she needs
nothing but epic
stillness in morning
where breakfast is
to dreams as
quiet
is to all the love
in waves
broken over a
jagged inhospitable
shore
and her storms were
her own

The Mystery of Some Sighs

through a window
where
her shimmering
piles-up against him
with the scattered
newspapers
and mannequins
looking on
—here
there's death
by 1000
undeliverable
caresses

Get Your News In German for Maximum Effect

¿Will you be perusing the museum
today?
the woman at the ticket counter
asked
No
I said
Marauding the museum
so she handed me a lance
and a map of the building
and grounds
then a small man in his 70s
appeared holding a clipboard
This is Claude
The woman said
He'll be leading your tour
but at some point you'll
likely usurp his authority
and lead the tour yourself
throwing away your map and
using your baser instincts
to guide you
¿What do I do with him in that case?
I asked
As you see fit
She said
then Claude said
Right this way please
and I fished through my
pockets for supplies and
found 2 quarters
1 nickel
and a penny

Waking in Co2

perfectly
we stand
in the rain
without the novelty
of standing in the rain
worse—we were carrying
toasters in the rain
and looking for places
to plug them
in

(so there was that tension
for all our scissor-clutching
mothers)

and the cliché dogs
were at it again
we fandangoed the dead
we apologized
for the profusion
of our apologetics

now every time a kid feels
an adult emotion or we applaud
comedy instead of laughing
another spaceship leaves
the atmosphere carrying
a piece of the atmosphere
inside it
and away

The Visitor

There's a machine outside
that says it's the ghost of Carl Sagan
and would like to talk to you
He said
Tell it I'm busy making violins
out of all the trees Carl said he had
so much in common with
She said
You've changed
He said
there was a time you would have given
my left arm to have one conversation
with Carl
She didn't answer him
so he thought of
unvisited museums
and how some crying
can sound like laughing
I grew up
She said finally
you didn't
So you don't like Carl anymore
He said
He's disappointing
She said
I never knew you thought that
He said
I didn't want to disappoint you
She said like someone
dissecting a seed for him to
learn something about seeds
—upstairs
the moon
tired of the poems
sick with swelling words.

It's Like This:

Someone speaks
  all flowers-and-sunshine
  then storms everyone in the place
  with rain/sleet/suicide
  like boring gray rocks
Someone chisels god-words in stone
  then breaks-out the jackhammer
  and it's all powder-for-substrate
  for another road to gone-missing-ville
Someone bricks out a path
  o-fool's-gold
  to the land of Oz
  then flying monkeys
  and we never get to know
  the other witch—just her curled-feet
(somehow I fell in love with her)

 Someone all sweet-cheese
  and blueberry
      now
    and yes
    and kisses tied in twine
but
    no
just no because—

 and we're bricked-offed
 by the la-la-la's
  by the I-can't-hear-yous
 right up there with
 the Dowager of Tuesday morning
 the Emperor of Sunday night
  everybody wins a ribbon for best loser
 we're all rickety-stringed-things
 one eye on eternity
 one hand on the lever of dip-shit
          doom

Modesty

she wore
a wool

tunic

in the
panic

of the
Punic

wars

The Actual Sea

as opposed to the finest
in gold-plated dildos
or the last fiberglass
dinosaur in Ohio

the actual sea
a masterpiece behind
3 poker-playing dogs
and visited finally

by some corn-fed idiot
sinking
an ache in the tooth
soul
spotless

Some Things that
Happen While a King
Oversleeps

someone will wash the blood
from their armor and find
a better God

someone will draw a bow
and release the most
beautiful music

someone with only
one breath left will fill it
with icy water

a woman will drape a beast
over her shoulder and waltz
from one empty room
to another to music
only she hears—while
a pale moon hangs dumb
in a blue sky
the one the sun
will push off to night
and take all the credit
for daylight's stupid
gleaming

Superhero

Who couldn't music
or dance
who argued mountains
to flat
who was a garbage truck
overflowing with
broken violins
who stupids before
television
who crashed the piano
flowering
an accidental chord
so beautiful
the world's weeping is heard
on Mars
who is a father
but cannot father
like an Atticus
who is no excellent horse
who doesn't afraid about you
who makes grand gestures
of flair
whose audience arrives
on foot
and leaves in helicopters
whose one and only good
shoe stays
a beast forever
who is an apology machine
grinding down
memory
and done

Bored / No Skillz

I saw her like
absolute flames

across the Museum
of Otherwise Wistful Portraits

and the world doesn't budge
at this—

I can claim nothing tumultuous
in me—a table to lay a calendar on

find the golden age of something
television missed and mark it

in pencil—wait

for any historian to arrive
and start talking me to sleep

You Are Not Buffalo

You are not Poughkeepsie
you are not in Poughkeepsie
not in a documentary
about Poughkeepsie

You are not ire and bleak
not overtly ample or humble

You are not seething with
anything

You are not mountain
or any geography
you are not food for thought

You are not folded and blessed
into any wallet

You are not freezing quietly
to yourself
you are not reminding us
what you don't need
so we can keep it from you

You are not spring with guffaws
and slaps on backs
you are not kingdom
not English hesitation

You have some name
made of words I arrange
in me
like a cluttered
fucked-up basement

My Excellent Horse's Race is Run

It isn't that he talked but
that he talked too much
and all that excellent talk
cost him place after place
and all my winnings
—worse
my excellent horse spoke
in easy to debunk accents
and gave long answers
to questions no one even asked
worse
while prattling on and on
he took the circuitous route around the track
he emphasized the need for frequent breaks
during his race for better health
and laughter as a tonic
and so the bad jokes
by race's end my excellent horse
had a view of the field
in ruins—I could hardly make out
his most excellent apology
this time in a German
(or was it an Austrian)
accent
(I think)

Weather Report

I could rain on anything
He said
but
those hoop-earrings
throw my strato-nimbus aground

I'm surrounded
by ardent dogs
She said

I can rain on that
He said

Maybe
She said
if you weren't some white-whaled
sin-soaked something-or-other
        un-built
     un-on
        extra
      eternally
   un-
     arrived

But i'm here
He said
look at the barometer

You're a braille edition
She said
decipherable
     only
     and ever
     and if even

by hands

He looked down
at the oven mitts
she wore like a boxer

Never Trust a Heartsick Trombonist
Sitting at a Piano to Do the Right Thing

His fingers will lie all over the keys
like some avant-garde typist with
nothing to say

He'll say it anyway

If rhythm comes out of this
avoid nodding your head

No one named Nunzio would do this.

And you have better things to do
and none of them involve
tumbling down a well
for the sake of a fool who
would turn your feelings to mulch
for his garden of grief
and tiny tornadoes

His heart is crumpled and
it would take a deaf person
with a keen eye to get that

Step outside all this and listen
for something real

An oboe played by a cartographer
gently parts the air

The Failure of Music

She whispered
the sound of a jet
departing

she sent him
an envoy
with her signature on
a rickety ceasefire

She returned in red
in sleep and
like a storm

He could only
lash himself
to a mast

Until she sirened him
back to his senses
—a Walsingham
riding a unicycle
to her Majesty

Contrition Contortion

sorry about the helicopters
and the other stuff
    the BlackOps thing
extraction
to another universe
(sorry 'bout that too)
(she said she'd make it up to you
in flamenco)
(in doughnuts dipped in whiskey)

sorry
for introducing her
your toothless/mockingbird

                                        smile
sorry about that
              the most

Of a Feather
or
Before the Spooning

Don't come near me
She said from the
other side of the door
I smell like a dumpster
I have no joy in me
And I'm tired
so he walked for 1000 miles
and presented his sad
dusty shoes to her and asked
¿This tired?
Yes—She said
he screwed
Rachmaninoff into
his ears for hours
presented himself
weeping in D minor 7th
to her and said
¿This sad?
Yes—She said
he put his broken
heart on a platter
of food and threw it
into a dumpster
behind a 5-star restaurant
then rummaged around
for days to retrieve it
¿This smelly?
He asked

Yes—She said
and she invited him inside
to sit with her among
shards of ostraka
handed him some glue
rearranged the pieces
to make a place
to nest— and after counting
and laughing about
everyone they loved who
wasn't lucky enough to be them— slept

Far from Rome

Walking around like
a shoulderless Emerson
head dragging on a memory
followed by a flock
of whispering violins

shoes like Novocaine
penicillin clouds
all the passers-by
with airplane smiles
every other car offering a ride

every other—other car
With a body in the trunk

you can side-eye this fact
but you know it
you put them there

but this is a poem
so you didn't really

?In all your years
Have you ever
(In real life)
heard anyone
use the word *Crystalline*?

No
you may say without thinking
because you don't live
in a poem
you live where it counts

in a book

about a barn
oddly of stone

A Gathering of Awkwards

—Well Bless His Heart
said the tallest
woman
in the assembled
crowd of
Ladies and Gentlemen
as she held aloft the
swaddled package
like a game show attendant
—¿How will we remember him
after he's gone?
—¿
She asked mid-atlantic-like
the questions went on
like this forever
without answers
so no one could grow old

Kind of
In a Way
On a Bridge

spanning from
fog to fog
you're all walking and
no progress and
it's raining leaflets
with pictures of you
described as gone
missing while trying
to cross a long bridge
in the fog—the one who
didn't listen—
and on the back are
advertisements for
banjo lessons
for the less than fully-
fingered
but you still have
all your fingers for
drumming the song
of where you forgot
you were going and
someone might have been
following behind but
has given up on you
and the railings are
more and more
inviting
tied to nothing
all the walking
wasted and
all the denunciations
of your odyssey

translated into
16 languages
following you
there's the railing
—you could fly

She-Thief in Natasha Boots at the Museum

All that talent

that singular
wit
charm
and beauty

is nothing

against even a
half-demented,
half-determined
custodian on duty

if you insist on wearing
those sexy-clumpy things

For *You*

You know someone
—a relation you think but
you can never be sure
how distant—how close
with all those radio waves
and storm warnings in the air

Who makes paper airplanes
of fake feelings and flings them
in your face

Who straps on the largest
wheels and runs over
the small-wheeled people

Who shuts off all the water
then digs-up all the clams
just to taunt them

¿You know how the smell
of gasoline is a thing?
like how your friend
—the one who took a blow
to the head and hates
the smell of bacon now—
(¿can you still call them kindred?)
finds nothing pleasantly silly
anymore
and listens to the news
on a shortwave radio
lying on a bed of nails

It's Bound to Be Complicated

Like how a guy named
Olaf gently shows you
the secret to decoding
runes before he runs you
through with a giant
rune-engraved sword
or
the cards you'll spend
a lifetime learning so
you can beat that certain
someone at their own
game—then when you
finally sit across
from her to play
she wins by default
because you just die
because the true meaning
of spending a lifetime
learning anything means
that your life ends when
you finally do

2.
Everytime you roll your eyes
an angel gets the axe

3.
I don't have a favorite
chair anymore—
She'll say
I don't enjoy complexity
like I think I might have
You'll say

Here is a better life loved
through confusion
You'll both agree
Let the Dead Bury the Dead
Said a movie
It's complicated
The Universe whispers
Don't ask.

Breakfast with Mom

She's 92 and she looks great
Mom continued

Ok
I said

She lives with her son who
hangs deserters from the circus
for a living
and her husband invented
a thing to inflate those things—
¿what do you call them?

Detachable hopes and dreams.
I said

No—she said
that would be weird
—This is a thing to help with finding the
answers to all the Jeopardy questions
—but it inflates ¿you know?

ok
yeah
I know
I said
Like the thing dad bought
at the yard sale for the criminally insane—¿right?

¿What?—Anyway
While she was telling me
about her husband
who was dead

her eye loosened-up
—¡she's 94!
so I said she should get it tightened-up
at the doctor's but she waited too long
and it just fell out—
¡WELL you can imagine how all the girls laughed!
I guess it's horrible really ¿huh?

Yeah
I said

But I missed the last part—
Something about eggs
I think

The Violins are at the Door

They say they want tears they say
if they don't get them they'll send
for an oboe and maybe a soprano
with an aria as big as the sky
and I think what it took
just to walk past a post office
avoid mailing myself away
enter a bank and withdraw
another memory of her
smell of bread and sweet
sweat—that glistening
of tiny beads on her face
because the ac wasn't keeping
up—but I wanted it to be my
weather system to blame
and to blame for the smirk
of a lover whose love's meaning
is to part my ribs and point there
singing in a slippery tongue
There's a liver where a heart
should be —
Once I said
¿Could I borrow and burn
that oboe in your breast?
—Just in case
and she's suspicious at this
and I can hear them tuning-up
outside and I feel a church growing
around me to keep her out
but I'd prefer her be able to visit—
stay awhile and grow something
for her bare feet to walk softly on

There Should be a Parable

that would explain what moves
inside you like a crowd
of people mulling around
trapped
at a bad party

But there isn't that story
there's only awkward
silent
moments shaped like fish
no one
would eat

The light is green now
the drivers behind you
honk and holler and
you howl-back like a broken
Grendel because no one sees
the goose-stepping chihuahua
crossing in front of you—

¿and what do they want you
to do
run the little fucker over?

Godzilla, the Jaws of Life, and JD Salinger's Big Mistake

Somewhere
a bevy of Japanese scientists
working in sweatless ardor
on some secluded island are
sciencing-out solutions
to the problem of her
"I'm leaving"
sung piano-piano

But to be present in the world means
knowing there's no way
they've arrived at anything
other than the weeping of violins
and the distressed moaning of cellos
as the Visigoths crest
the seventh hill
we smile-stupid-and love
like a thousand Julys
have descended upon us

She walked—
and the rest of us are only
late to the party of one-sided
conversation

We've gained
nothing
from all that museum-going

Rapport,
A Bad Cowboy Story

(In the voice of Sam Elliot)

Some blue thing of me
swings from a tree
—my last thought
was 'bout
my mount
shot out
from under my ass
so long ago now
I don't remember his name
but he was a good horse

them days we rode everywhere—
Egypt-even
—saw a sphinx
—met some Pharoahs
(as I recollect)

and all the arrows
missed
and the sabers swung
wide
and we dodged all the lead
—except that last ball

but I got the sonofabitch good
for that— laid him out
flat
with one shot

then I took his horse
sold 'em in the next town
for a buck
his name was Amigo
and we had no rapport
at all

Played Ragged Maps to No Place

played wailing mountains flat

played brace of wood against water

played triumphant sword-wielding heroine

played search and came to gut retching

played once then never Ouija again

played Europe and dashing

played therapeutic Steve McQueen

played telephone-specific rage

played them all for crying

played armoring justice

played grim wretched morning

played mattress death till afternoon

played muffled underwater song

played television long goodbyes

played faraway east and cold expanse

played mink and bread and telescopes

played standing stupid random idea

played astral-plane of forever

played she walked in notions

played deft and shining judgments

played another stretch of day gone to night

played so far away it hurts

The Ungulate

I.
A stairway is not a tunnel
(per se) she said
and he said
Yours are not the guts
that will grease the tracks
of any war machine
of mine

so satisfied and smiling they
—with a claxonmouthed
clown as sherpa—
clacked-off in their steel
rhinoceroses
to the zoo
to battle with the keepers
to keep
the snow leopard cubs from growing up and out
of what they are
and into the world

II.
Ray-guns and diners
are the same thing
(per se) he said
and she said
You'd not be the one I'd humiliate
in a stadium filled with
idiot archetypes

and so no words
like wasps between them
and where once they

knee-deep in cranberries
now is a choice of excavation
every shovelful is music
or money
or sometimes neither
but never both
Nowhere was a country
and Nothing a name
worth penning

III.
Her face —
—he voyaged for it

IV.
She explained the
movement of her feet
as "walking"
and the space she moved
through as
"/ˈTHerəpē/"

—he adjusted his understanding
of her to include the word
"exclusive"
and built a single-entry
encyclopedia for her to inhabit
she took him up on it
invited him in
and he stayed

V.
All outside
was Oslo and snow

(per se)
inside was all a giraffe
gentle and dying

I'd kill this thing for you
she said
I kill this thing for *you*
he said

and so they were warm
in the company of that lonely
—and increasingly nervous
animal

VI.
One thousand years
passed

VII.
A story is not
a tunnel (per se)
we say

theirs are not the clothes
we emerge in
—mottled furs
  from a dead innocent

one reluctant
to let the other's eyes
do all the seeing now

the other
reluctantly/tonguelessly
cedes all the talking now

¡What a pair!
(per se) we say
¿see?
winter is over

You Can Be Less Shy in French

You can
—stare
(in French)
unabashedly
at a line of
forthright
cherry toes
and
all that
is stacked
above them
—imagine
(in French)
the tips
of your fingers
falling
(gliding Frenchly)
from lips
to neck
while
—holding
a book
in your
free hand
and
—reading
(in English)
how to pronounce
(in French)
the word
you can't
—remember
now
to describe
the taste of

blood
from the lip
you bit
trying to
—mouth
that ultra-
polysyllabic
word
(in German)
to describe
the shock
of chainmail
on skin
before you
—declare
(in Portuguese)
the conquering
of some
land
or other
for a green-
eyed trobairitz
—bent
on singing
the ghosts
back
before
the fires
that made them
and it's not
that you don't
—care
(in French)
it's just
all Greek
to you

Allies

The war was over
and we weren't supposed to
fraternize with the locals but
she was the kind of beautiful
most other people call attractive
and so much so I couldn't look
into her eyes for very long because
that felt like falling down a well and
besides she was a Mussolini-loving
fascist, or that was what they said
about all the zaftig women around
here but I chose not to buy that,
and she had a cat named Fupa that
she said I could pet and it wasn't until 1947
that I found out what fupa meant and
that gave me a chuckle one morning in 1949,
alone, in bed, while I listened to Dvořák's 9th
which never worked for me because
the 2nd movement was too American,
too sad, so I waited for the 3rd but
that starts too marshal and transitions
into something too pastoral for
stroking anything but a cat so I just
gave up and lay there remembering
how she trapped me under all that
grinding fascism until the sun said
no to all that. Now Mahler's 5th is on the radio
and it doesn't even occur to me to swell.

Anthem of the Weird

Eamon ran amuck
oh, Yeamon you drill like cyclops!
She said
so hero, he wept, ego-blistered-ire
a-topped, a-spinning eye-opia
shinny-him desperate mob-eternal
on unkempt, rhythmic, old-odalisque
he-eye, him float, they fly, oh nap!
(incoherent now, he quit!)
and what-waiting sun
-breaks
to blind an eye
and lame-a-leg or two…
so hero
he wept
so hero
he slept
and sleeping
and weeping
and wanting

so hero
he long ago
gone-dead

In Scheherazade's Sister's Bed

His mind (lost) drifts
over her landscape

The salty sweat

From the small
of her back

On his lips

She turns away on her side
Boredom-eyed

Glancing
over her shoulder

At his predicament

If she moves
he's done for

If he moves
he's done for

She yawns knowing
he'll break out laughing

And who doesn't shake
with laughter?

Regnum Defende

Imagine—
There's a song playing
so good it deserves
its own playlist
and the parking is like
a confusion of dories
at the end of a whale
slaughter and you're running
up stairs dodging tumbling
household appliances thrown
by the god of mini-fridges
and you're trying like hell
and a wheezing Neruda
to warn her before
that morning star
catches you
but you can only
manage inch-long
words exhaled like
regrets you didn't know
you had till now
and whispered
in the wrong ear
but this is a dream
—you think
or at least a perfect
James Bond movie
and the moral is simple—
it's possible to hold
a monarchy in contempt
and still love a queen

How Best in Bronze
to Show Your Feelings
for Her

1.
Organize words into
tiny armies to invade
the shores of her
consciousness

2.
Hold your head
in your hands and
roll it up some
Sisyphean hill
named—Here is Where
the Hopeless Sigh

3.
Sigh

4.
Carve an immovable
statue of her

5.
Get used to it until
she shows up
carrying her
love
and a jackhammer

Somewhere Else a Feast

while I came home
to find the kitchen faucet
drooling and
the drains all stubborn

the television still warm
with rage
a ceiling peeling

in despair
all the wallpaper unyielding
the oak floor sighing
the couch having rescinded

all invitations
and the mail was trying hard
for menace from the floor
all the books were mocking

and my favorite chair
could only creak
suicide
the pantry held

little promise
the fridge was mesmerizing
but gave up nothing
the clocks tried hiding the truth

the doorframes said
Move along
every wall said
Sleep—

just not here

The Chance Quartet

after Brendan MacCallister's painting First Supper

The Chance Quartet of Berlin
wash violins
cellos and violas
in the tears of their
disappointed mothers

Then gather backstage like
busted-up
brahmans bent on telepathic
grumbling and the music of chance

One inhaled the purple off flowers
and refuses to exhale

One peels everything off today
to stick to tomorrow

One throws a tantrum of smeared
silence and transparency

One is refusing to give up the balcony
and is threatening to become a god

In the program this is called
mottenzerfressen or the
Moth-eaten-waiting-for-
something-to-flower-prelude
and takes days and decades

So there are only two
left alive in the audience
—waiting

Hands like spiders stitched
together

They fancied themselves
a couple before
the waiting broke something
between them

They stopped talking
the same language
years ago
they forgot the sun

2 fools
waiting
on 4 idiots
to get their act
       together
fold
and play them back to
to where they started

Mid-Century Art Show W/Bullets

that chair really helps the world
forget the last war

thanks for the ALL CAPS revelation
about Whitman
his machine gun
his sidekick
the aviator X

thanks for the explanatory zeal
all the pointy
pitchforks were a fine way to say it
and the execution was a relief really
and the fire a nice touch
the flame-proof ideas
falling like tiny crows
after the ropes burned away

so all our backbones make a church

thanks for introducing
our Lord Protector over memory
who captained and scarred us
from further wanting

too late now I'd have paid the orchestra
a century's-worth of longing
for that music

instead
find book-length winging
for each triumph in tenths

Love Means Never Having to Distinguish Between the Sound of a Clarinet and the Sound of a Crying Baby

A grandmother undoes loneliness
with the pyramids at Giza

and a miniature orange tree

She married a radio and withered a flag

She drove a car as big as the US space program
without hesitation

Her acreage was obscene

soft in summer

in winter a place for a dog
to wander and die in

Everything merged with her bank account

She imported Christmas from Germany

¿Did you find the bomb shelter behind the house?
she asked

And I answered by suffocating

Every Time a Wink,
a Crow Dies

Horribly

in the mud

once black wings

covered

in a slip of Earth

desperately clawing

for a grip of atmosphere

—finding only the vacuum

                    of bad metaphor

Soiree

Across a crowded room
he motioned to her
in broken semaphore
¿How do you feel?
and luckily she had written
a 900 page book
the night before
explaining why
she couldn't explain
how she felt and
so she mailed it to him
packaged with some
crudités from a sad
platter on her side
of the the room
and when it arrived
on his side
the party was over
the guests having shrugged
themselves to indifference
and disappeared in a
haze of ennui and
disappointed sex
leaving them a vast
and empty space
they could finally wander
across as lonely nomads
and find each other—
read her book together
and agree that the weather
inside them was the same

Snow

He ran out of heat
dreaming counterfeit
memories of
goodbye
goodluck
Godspeed
before
strapping on
ampersand shoes
for a failed
expedition
in search
of a safety pin
to close the subject
as he froze
thinking
Hoop earrings—
I remember
hoop earrings
¿And what
He asked himself
Do you count yourself
the master of?

Lost Like Music

—uncaged
she oceans her way into my
dark and tiny opera of night
while I was wondering
when exactly talking to pets
becomes a pathology or
whether it's worth calling
a soul A Soul with all the
war-making that can bring—
I glide over her heart
until the resonance of her words
up from under her ribcage
washes me up onto morning
more or less like all mornings
and all the days before when
forfeit rolled over fortune
and days pile-up in a place
built of cut-up travel magazines
and unopened cans of can openers
and this is how new ideas for cooking
shows die on the vine—how
floral prints make their way
in the world attached to someone
who is otherwise dead and crying
—now a gentle minotaur
is at the door
like water perfectly flowing
the beast has flowers and
and a message—
—Whatever isn't boring
is worth doing like a stevedore
emptying a heart's cargo

Something Beautiful Under Ice

Like meeting a
bad guy
who breathes daisies
for you
to walk on
and you'll think—Weird
—But not a bad guy
¿because how could you know
he just came from
drowning someone's
philosophy or
knocking someone off
their tricycle of artistry?
—always that one squeaky
wheel

How to Fake a Fake Orgasm

—Have a real one
by conventional means
use pages of the dictionary
to make a paper mâché lover
for conversational foreplay
about the decline of mud
shrimp using words
that would break a horse
in two over a meal of
date night Tuscan ravioli
salted with the tears of
your shared enemies
who you hate for making
you into boring reactionaries
—be the one the gods squint at
then retreat outsmarted
by undone memories
—be raffish
because
what is caged
uniquely cannot happen

¿Why Would We End...

When we can't really see each other
for all the fuss about our role in
undoing the last century

It's like a castle with arms
too weak to hold in the inhabitants

Or a storm too strong to get across
its meaning so a wagon train
just stays wet with boredom
waiting for entertainment
to be made of the bitter end
it could have had if
it had the good sense to
go all dramatic with famine and blood

It's like we jumped without realizing
our parachutes needed to be coerced
into opening with whispers of
sweet nothings

For extra optimism we try reading
the words "personal tragedy" as
"one custom-crafted tragedy for us alone"

There's a fuck-you Moon absorbing
all our praise for its beauty
while strangling the sun from rising

There's a parking job gone so bad
it makes the news

Something to cry about finally

Waves and plagues

It's like dancing poorly for a legless audience

Bent

On pity for us

Barbara Bain's 1st Husband

There was a theory in
Bone Reading Class that
Martin Landau's whole
reason for being was to be
mistaken for some other actor
after his death
Like we're supposed to
keep saying
¿Isn't that Martin Landau?
or
Let's screw till our eyes glaze
over and forget to
finish the job because Martin
Landau might almost be
in that movie in the other room
or
¿Won't there always be more
to acting than just a group of
mouths smashing words together?
¡Martin Landau didn't do that!
and
¿Didn't Martin Landau captain
an obdurate moon and wasn't that
worth a seat at the table
of the /ˌidēosiNGˈkradiks/ club?
—These are real questions

And there will be those
who want to profit off this
c0nFusioN—split it
like atoms for fuel to launch us
all into a miniseries about
finally getting to mars and deafen

us with whispered rumors
that the olde world *was*
a stage
and Martin Landau was
around every corner

Greenhouse Effect

It's someplace to go
to escape the dry air of
all the shopping mall zombies
exhaling about all the next things
to do

About you—like
Shouldn't we make guns
out of her snark?
Or
Me
Why not spin him into
a superhero named Clem
the Jaunty?

You pass through the glass
door and feel better
immediately —if you
are a flower, or
my flower type

I'd say we win

The greatest legal minds
melt here

Demons are cosmically not allowed here

The worst endings to bad stories
park here —turn like faces
gently forced to look at the afternoon
outside

If Found to Be Unholy
Tell Them I Was Never Here

Tell them —after all
the correct appreciation of
architecture is a mailman tripping
over a skateboard
and that
the right feeling
at the distance
of small houses
stiffens the pen
—dooms us
to be uniquely
alone

À l'Atelier des Visages

¿where was all this
light
before her ugly shoes
walked in?
now he's hanging
like loose clothes
from a shrinking frame

—somewhere a Spanish
guitar rings a reminder
and he pulls her into
a memory
where
her belly
growls into his ear
—Don't break this love
he dreams back
—Ok

There's a Shark in the Pond with a Guitar

there's a drink held like
a grenade at a bad cocktail party

someone loves your life but
hates the font it's written in

there's autumn looking like
it wants to murder spring

a woman named Alex would
prefer you leave the card table

some flowers are whispering
the name of your next dead relative

it's acoustically crowded inside
a head with sighing singers

somewhere a book
on a shelf is awaiting

the one who might have
understood the author best

never arriving—held up
with stage 4 ennui

alone
and anyway—illiterate

Dulcinea's Hemline

you paint like Turner—
the one: "Fishermen at Sea"
but
there are no fishermen
no sea
just that breezy
insanity of love
driven wild
a slow moving
sandstorm of a sky
and us without camels
it is an undone and forlorn
thing:
your
No
your
I've got to go
our train huffing
at the station
the strange thing
about loving that
feeling of loving
that turns
and bites us in the ass
and there's us without
the double-stitch
to keep us from Romeo
and Juliette-ing ourselves
into a raging sea
where fishermen
are fucked
under a Turner sky

Extra Rhapsodic

Until you really look at it
like a party filled
with people too challenging
to behold properly
because you're standing
in the middle of all of it
on a rickety tea chest
screaming about the benefits
of enthusiasm like a whale
breaching the surface
of an ocean of indifference
while someone is digging your
grave quietly
in a dimly lit backyard
and so you have to leave
that party and go to some
broom closet of a space
where a tiny population
of vacuum-pushers and
spoon-swirlers in awkward
fitting clothes congratulate
each other cuz \'rē-zⁿns\
and you notice they're digging
graves too
just not yours
not yet
for now they smile
and almost welcome you

The Aside

Michelangelo got it wrong
She said
You should get it right—
and while the rest of the
party tried for conversation
a thousand birds flew
between them
she carved him
into words
for future arguments
then
they rejoined
the party
him still at sea
she
a library on shore
all her books unread

The Thing (is)

after Brendan MacCallister's painting, AM

You look like an oddly rendered
executioner
She said
Well there's a dark
and inconceivable thing
only a string quartet could get at
He said
We could hire one
She said
Or we could just release the one
we've had in the basement for
years and have them play for us
He said
You forgot to feed them
She said
They resorted to cannibalism
there's only one left
Jesus
He said
now I feel really bad about that
We all make mistakes
She said heading down cellar
and he instantly felt better
maybe that was love
He thought
someone lovingly lifting the guilt
off someone's shoulders
an absolutionist
that's her—that's love
Here's the soloist
She said sitting a well-fed cellist
in front of them

and the musician improvised
beautifully but alone
and it was all back on his shoulders again
he looked over at her
this time she only shrugged
anything she could say against
that music was held up on a train
outside of town

45

Crooked-footed
bent
baleful
beast with creak
and wail
wizened-headed
gamy legs crashing
up some 10-lane
boulevard
spots and stripes
a thunk stuck
in some old fold
of Brioni

Got breakfast
backward
misunderstood
lunch
declared war
on supper
made boredom
out of jealousy
pronounced every word
            upside down
     listened
   like no one's business
to anyone

East

She is a new and
snarky world

And I owe some
god or other

Thanks

Who blew her hair
from her neck
That land cleared

She invited me
to stay a while

Visit
come close
and kiss the ground

High Praise

I really liked your
massive parade
I agree with your
findings
and the experiment was
rad
your job of conducting
really
made the orchestra
seem like an empire

you've won
and in
winning
proved
talent
is an Odysseus
hare-brained
and mapless

Declaration

Begin as you mean to go on
She said
Good one
Let's get interested in something
He said
let's invade Poland
Let's give France such a look
She said
and that's how it was
they stumbled into the next hour
tumbled
into the next day and careened
into the years ahead
while some events of upside-down-did
and happenings-because-they-couldn't-be-
helped—didn't
they:
eventually-amazed-and-therefore-
thinking-long-gones-and-ever-impossibles

and in the end it was like this:
she made her way in an orange freight-car
to Alaska under the bluest sky
he—let's call him forgetful—
hired the smoothest driver to follow
that he could die slowly in the backseat
his last thoughts all blue with orange

O Fado

¿Religion?
He wondered
boringly earnest
after she flashed that
snapshot
from planet X
where all the fake nuns go
for drinks
and talking shit
about how a future her
would bring him
to some brink of himself
with the dark of her eyes
the smirk of her
lips mouthing the words
as cold as a detour
to desire
so he changed the subject
in his chest
to something more benign
like war
or polio
or what it must be like to
kiss the ground under
a tall bridge
or
how
one crescendo wouldn't
do
(or two) he knew
to undo the day
so he reached
for another but

settled for the brink
while
from behind a telescope
on planet X she lied
Red is a warrant
Do something
         do anything
You dopey heathen

The Losers

We lost to the rain
the rain lost to the sun
the sun lost to the moon

We are shot-through
pleasure-unhinged

We're firetrucks at the opera
gin-soaked gun-toters

Leaning Grouchos, stepping
Gomorrah-bound beasts

The world floods-up under us
we'll lose—we'll drown

We winged-things will go flightless
and spiral with no place to land

Stellar Stella

Who traded-in her Volvo
for a hovercraft and
parks it like Al Capone
who renames colors
after historical events
that haven't happened
(yet) hacks passwords
of the rich and famous
just so she can give them
new ones with exclamation
points and hidden meanings
the rumor of her face
on canvas launched
a thousand ships filled
with art critics and
meter-maiden-bounty-hunters
who landed like disappointed
amphibians finding no
"Wanted for Wanton Parking"
posters—and "Stellar Stella"
the critics cried—
would've rivaled
"Momentous Mona (Lisa)"
—If only
she would have assented

The Next to Last Day

It's all so uninteresting
it might as well be Tuesday morning
all those tiny Japanese trees dreaming of home
today's skullduggery of empty things
black dragon tongues
flame licked
the clouds
last night
the sun gone missing for weeks
the space left in the world in your wake
now I'm heart attack awake
and clanging out
into the world
where hearts
strap on stilts
and high-stride the day to pieces
they witch their way over others
over the bent-backed
—smiling

T-Minus

I.

That space suit
makes you look old
She said
I'll make up for it in swagger
He said
You'll burn up on reentry
She said
I'm only going to the
supermarket
He said
Still...
She said
All the produce has gone bad
and nothing is on sale anymore
......

Yeah
He said stepping out and under
the stars just showing
their tiny
stupid faces
he fingered the small hole
in his T-shirt (accusingly)
That was enough
He thought
She's right

II.

What to Take

.....
¿What did you do with all

the humor
She said
It was falling short and
asleep
so I pushed it off the couch
He said
¿And all the leftovers?
She said
Unimpressive
He said
so I fed them to the last fish
in the last aquarium
in the last city
¿Did you pack the cat?
She said
The cat's been dead
for over a year
He said
I know
She said
¿Did you pack him?
Yes
He said
edging closer to the door
outside
the sun so small now
the sky could ignore it
stay black
and cradle the future
against the past
trees and all.

Blessed
You Think, Until You Don't

Because somewhere
a Titanic sunk but no one
thought to make a movie about it

Because whole worlds
that never made it
out of post-production

Because fragile actors
Pompeii'd while grasping
for syndication or
licensed action figures
at least

Because roads built
to driveways leading to
houses no one ever visits
that everyone talks about
in whispered German sighs

Because someone chokes
on the word OUTLANDISH
in an aristocratic southern accent
clutching something lacey

How Should I Tell It

¿Weightlessly—
you anchor me to dumb sleep
and your stare overflows
and your laugh overflows
and it seems you know more
than a god of neurology
because something dreaming in you
is dreaming in me
and the night turns serious
and you lift away from me so slowly
I wonder if there's an elegy for this
formally forgotten feeling
I reach to pull you back
(¿didn't you promise
to help translate something?)
I find nothing but waking
I'm only a shore without water
nothing glistening
nothing worth walking to

The Paradise of the Banal

(Or, What Would it be Like to be Eaten
by a Tribe of Garden Gnomes?)

¿You know like
when you're about 10 years
olde
and you pretend to be British
by using a British accent
to the real British lady
who lives
mysteriously
down the street
and she asks through
her smiling
obviously real
particularly British teeth—
"What part of England are you from?"

And then all the buildings
inside you collapse
and the bridge to your
certain adulthood
is swaying too so
now even that is in doubt
and you feel like you're wearing
a forsythia-print snow parka
at a parade in July?

Well—
It's like that.

The Cage

Some lowercase "g"od
un-seriously demanded
a ceremony of journalists
be unleashed on a city
within a city built in honor
of all the fallen tarpaulin
salesmen who fled to
Tahiti and never looked back
and populated with every
impressionistic depiction
of Joan of Arc come to life
each out-doing each other
with insane proclamations
and sword-waving at the
journalists who found
themselves rudderless in
a sea of otherwise non-events
until the smallest of them
wriggled through the irony
of it all and brought news
of this to me wherein I
dropped what I was pretending
to be doing and followed
the little man to the center
of all controversy where
there was this one Joan—
The Joan of Snark and
where art dances spinning
on one leg claiming more
than its worth to the applause
of the credulous and the
showering of slanted gifts
and as if I needed more

fuel for my long-smoldering
she suggested a black satin
road map criss-crossing that
imagined topography to confuse
my sense of direction
—I had only suggested armor...

Strangle the Curator

the walls are a figurative
—blurry confusion
crush
the conductor's fingers
(and break his little
 stick)
the music has become
drunken and frothing
at the mouth
arrange
for the evisceration
of the architect
who allowed buildings
to get away with murder
be one of the unwashed masses
and stink to high heaven
till the maître d' says
¡go!
then flash
a fistful of fortune
and wink:
I think
I'll stay

then leave anyway

the squirrels are in charge
the horses were just boring
after all
and the pastry boxes
were only fooling
and empty on opening

it's /kən'sep(t)SH(əw)əl/
it's ok
we've been had

Frenemies' Ambush

She reserved a chair
for him to witness
the signing of his
own unconditional
surrender

Now some fugitive
thing in him undoes
his sleep and stays
unanswered—
he enjoys the warmth
of it anyway

From the Bottom of a Well
in Someplace Like Oslo

or from behind a closed door
at a secret-agent convention
comes whispering of bad weather

from a guy with a face cobbled-
together from papier-mâché cash
and awkward interviews

sometimes he sleeps like we do
and the low rumble of combustion
he dreams hearing is as fake
as an introduction to an audience
snowed-in in Montana
piped-in from Mars

On Writing

You live inside the best machine
She said
It's not so great
He said
I like your machine better

I don't live in a machine
She said
I live in a constant wedding

Well mine is an endless funeral
He said

I am tethered to nothing
She said
I am a four-legged beast
in a ballroom
She said with her teeth this time

Yes you are
He said
Lucky that way
He said

Outside there was only snow
where rain should be

They landed hard
and climbed out of their
conversation
like two cosmonauts
from a burning capsule

Honesty is a Machine
with Grasping Fingers

"Never write when
under the thrall of
the Virgin Mary"

—Said Neruda
Who ate bugs sprinkled
on his salad
and alive
The idea was to eat fast
enough that they wouldn't
get away

"Never be parenthetical
in your honesty"

—Said Joyce
Who drank shoe
polish diluted with
turpentine
and so went slowly
blind
and the letters on the page
moved away
from his intention

"Say the word
'Anatomy' into
a microphone during
a grain auction
to bring all the surrounding
churches crashing down"

—Said Sharon Olds

who will never
see this lie
like Christmas presents
in July

"Be a saucebox
while riding radio waves
like paisley narwhals
into the homes
of the unsuspecting"

—Said Tom Edison
who wore clothes so
stiff with the grime
of empire
he shown as bright
as a world's fair
he was uninvited to

(a notion
about something flowery
drinks air
from my lungs)

"Collect and analyze
all your Wednesdays
for future use"

—Said Rickover
Who pondered in tears everyone's
misunderstanding of him
every night in a
giant bed in a tiny house

I want someone in a movie
to say:

"Poetry is best recited
tumbling
down a well"

At some point
all jokes
are starved of oxygen
and a piano playing
makes us remember
everything
larger than it was large
smaller than it was small

We think we remember
oceans and deserts

That's how we know we're finished

ləˈk(y)o͞onə

I'm home
She said
But you're riding bareback
on an ostrich
—plus
you misplaced the
rent again
He said with a hint of cetology

You're always so
preoccupied with death
She said
—It's morose

You think you're so hot
He said

The Unctuous Tropical Fruit Drying
or
The Astronaut

and
there was the taste of lemon
she had in her
tears
cried
into my quinoa
the morning I was launched
careening
at the moon
carried as a child
some sickness in me
carried as a hero
doing the dying
into quiet
and God
and black
and God
and stars
and stars
and God
and quiet
the stars
and madness
the madness of contemplation
—turns out
the moon was no place
to strive for
to hunger for
to celebrate after all
at home we had gorillas
with their stupid miraculous curiosity

and avocados
and television
and dentistry
and nothing was more
brazen
with love

With Pineapples in Her Head

she took a banjo to the moon
debased it to barren rock
dressed it in stupid
and handed it over
to some dumb poets

and bells dangling
dumb in church tops
hung up their rung on a nail
and quit then and there

and things fall off other
          things

even the wallpaper
gave up the fight
and let go the wall
and sighed to the floor

she scribbled
the most moving eulogies
for those she ran over

she tutored fish
to walk a better sway

she had pineapples
in her head

she wrote streaky letters
leaky with love
to weedy downtroddens

she lived just long enough
to be beset by all manner
of maladies and

best them all to death
one by one

Essential Music for Necessary Sadness

Take all the
balalaikas
pulling their
sad Russian shit
till we sit like plants
—rainless
in undersized
cracked plastic pots
and stupid birds
pretty
pity us
from shining trees—
—take all that
to a medium-sized lake
and throw it in where
small meandering fish below
will breathe in the sadness
before being caught and prepared
and placed before the wizards of comfort
who pause before the tiny
icons in garnish
and mutter something of a prayer
to no God in particular
and tuck in

This—they will agree
is the taste of music.

The Corset and the Luchador

After Jennifer Toler's painting Verona

¿What's with the corset?
He asked her
I'm cranky
She said overflowing
the banks of her foundation
Well I have a match downtown
He said
She shrugged
It's with the ghost of
Enrique Ugartechea
He continued
She sighed like Dulcinea
and remembering her hands
rolling and crushing
the breasts of a virago
around him
wondered
if that would be considered
a hold or or a pin
You're not Mexican
She said
Kayfabe
He answered
Touché
She said
And you're not French
He said
inside
turquoise and gold reflections
surprised them to pieces
outside
the city ran like a demented clock

You know
She said pointing to the corset
I'm not wearing this for you
I know
He said pointing to his leotard
And I'm not wearing this for you
Of course
She said walking away
leaving him wandering a desert—
it was breakfast-o-clock
already
when he stepped into a sea
of fedoras—
realized
he'd lost another match

Instead of Sleep

She lives still like
the ghost of a sentinel
he could only have
by dragging
something of himself
out to die
and be carried off
like a waiter
clearing the table
while there's still
chewing going on—so
now he's an empty table
now he has guns for hands
there might still be music
in him
but she is her own
protector
her own orchestra—
he's just sniffing the air
alone
in the dark

The Shower

after Charles Bukowski
and Kenji Miyazawa

The weatherman called it

"Showers in the evening,
turning to heavy downpours
while standing naked in an alley"

He didn't say why only
in an alley

why the night would
host the phenomenon

why "naked"

or who with,
if anyone

So at around 7:30,
you stand in an alley
in a light rain, waiting

You strip to the waist
and feel the light pelting
on your shoulders, like

a thousand little angels
trying to get your attention
so you look up and get one

right in the eye
—she's not coming

that's what the universe
was trying to tell you

it was saying,
Look at you, you dope,
about to be naked in
the rain and losing.

Drenched with no one to share
the experience with

so you put your shirt back on
just as the sky opens up
and crashes down on your

now bare and stupid soul

And the weatherman called it
and you think,
Damn, how did he know?

His Muse in Repose Bewilders Him

If that song was waiting
to become the anthem
of his stupid
unmoored heart
it happened
when she lay her
smoldering exhaustion
before him—saying
            —Yes—
        and
        —Paint all of this—
but what he heard was
—I trust you—
and that was enough
for the former head of the department
of the once terminally unrelieved-in-love
-turned-Unknown-who-might-as-well
-be-on-the-moon to find a way
—finally
to lay his doubt
draped
like a spent flag over his shoulder
while he painted—and she left
leaving a space
to walk the streets
to commune with the oblivious cars
snuggled into parking spaces
    and satisfied for the night

¿How About This

¿How about you stop
being in a movie where

you look over your shoulder
at me in slow motion

to a sappy,
sad score played

on an electric piano?

¿How about get
a real piano
and play some Dvořák

on that thing?

That's all we need

¿How about the god
of dementia lighten-
up a bit

And give some good
memories back to
the elderly
and confused?

He can keep the bad
memories for bad movies
and ridiculous,
unavoidable operas

¿How about we all
stop with needing each
other so much, souls

swimming in
bad novellas, bad
poetry
badly
read

to the music
of anything you do
in slow motion

the light just
right?

¿How about that?

Vaseline
smeared
over whatever lens
we choose to see
the worst
of it
for the best reasons

The Godless Night Kitchen

Where day is overcooked
and blackened to night
and the wind comes drumming
a memory of the morning
while everyone else is sleeping
more soundly than you
your nimble fingers awake
at the abacus

We add up to something
like unwelcome religion
over and over again
And smiles are contraband
to each other
and in the morning you'll wake when
someone comes to you and
tells you the truth of what
an unfinished symphony
we are

And that a heart is designed
to harden and crack

There are birds in there

That's how they get out

Some Number of Mothers

Came together to sing about
the genuine genius of
their progeny
—like little Tommy
little Rebecca —like
Brandon's grades
enormous in their
predictive quality —how
Aaron's sister Francine
strangled him with language
and left him hanging from a
crying tree (and so on)
all the mothers came together
in music and a kind of slow
circling
and agreed this was worth
sending out for pizza
and wine
none of them wanted war
and the sorting could take a while

Seriously

and then
build your house
of cast-iron ribcage
and then
be better in the place
right before
you leave it
and then
speak in accents
and be mysterious
and then
drive with precision
and aggression
and then
you're European suave
and then
be languid
in the presence
of exciting things
and then
you're an unassailable
turtleneck sweater
and then
keep going on like that
and then
and then
and then
     be dead
and therefore
grass and sky
and then
(hopefully and by then)
they found you
way down in Mexico
a
legend

The Problems Show

There's only one path to God
she said
¿I think I know what you mean
Buffalo, New York right?
He said
No
She said
You have to stand naked
on the roof of an empty
parking garage and
check your wallet
like
really check it
(she made wonderful emphasizing noises)
If I'm naked
how do I check my wallet?
He asked
Where is it kept?
You know like when
you hear a piano
trilling some lounge music
behind a closed and locked door
in a building with no windows
She said,
And you just know someone's getting
strangled on the other side?
No, He said
I'm not a lounge-y person
He said
Well
there
in that feeling
folded and pressed into

your wallet
She said
You'll find the currency to
buy an audience with the Almighty
then
as if to put a finer point on it
she exploded into brilliance and light like
in the movies only
he was the only audience for this
effervescent punctuation
there was smoke too
and when the smoke cleared
he found he was in the pocket of God
with all the spare change of the world

The Phone Book of the Damned

Walking has that way
of moving your feet
closer to somewhere
other than where they started
and you follow along
helpless and unfolding
like a story your uncle told
about the zookeeper who was
talked into releasing the snow leopard cubs
by a strange couple with a pet giraffe and
then he joined a mariachi band
to escape justice
but you were too young
to feel the importance
of the story because
the zookeeper was just
THE ZOOKEEPER
so he was just A. Guy
riding his feet
walking away
nameless
unfolding
¿and could you have known
someday you'd meet
share a drink
find more easily than you
both thought possible
something to toast
raise your glasses
and trade names

Croustille de Mais

When we say we *like* the painting of
orangey junk food—(etc.)
what we mean is
we *want the real thing*—we're saying
the wind isn't enough to fill our sails

We're saying we need the coal
in the bunkers

We want bouffant —we say
but we say /bo͞o'fä/
like we know a thing or two about the French
Revolution as it relates to
something shiny to hold
when it arrives in the mail
and we just stare
'til our eyes
fall out and wake
the downstairs neighbors

We say we liked the poetry —readings—
but really we are saying we want to be
loved for rejecting the $hitforbrain food

We say—I'm sure of all this
take my hand
it's pronounced
/hand/
We'll do the useless things

we'll do them in the bad-ass style
like cowboys

Science fiction is calling our newly
chromed ears
is railroading our quality time—
that time that will foolish us

And the coiffure was huge
enough to make it more likely
we'll hit our heads on
the low-hanging fruit
but less likely we'll bruise
when we do

But we saw *that*
elemental logic coming

¿didn't we?

We read the fine print

We made the ridiculous our thing

We made Amazon our home

We say revolution
but we mean something paid for
kept in a drum or
a box or
the inside of someone we loved
now dead—
something blown-in from the cold
fallen from a tree
bathed in the banal

It belongs to me/us now
—we say
the rest of y'all can go hang

We know:

There is something about a windless
night blessed with the softest rain

And we can stand upright against
a wind of blown corn chips
after all—

Bird

¿What's with the raven?
She asked
He landed on me yesterday
while you were important
in New York
He said
—Amsterdam
She corrected him
¿What's he want with *you?*
She said
I think when I get small enough
he'll carry me away to Spain
He'll drop me on some vast
plain
where the Republic
had its last stand
against the fascists—
He'll tell me
You never did anything like this
And now it's too late
You're just small
and fruitless
He looked over at the bird
already flapping his wings
tugging at his shoulder
testing the weight
—He could have sworn
she had said New York

Or Eat What Would Kill a Dog

If your best interpretation
of the sign you're standing
dumb in front of in a strange
language is
—Make Caution Here
then assume
whoever hung it
didn't know what they
were talking about and
throw caution away from
the place you've always been—
head towards the icebergs and bayonets
riding a horse named Titan Nick and
start a war with any group
of 3 or more somebodies

Vast Hinterland of What

Where all the
grandfathers claim
they invented
steam
where all the sex
happens in
other people's
books about freedom
borrowed
and never returned
to less-than-moneyed
libraries no one
admits
exist
because the car
needs a transmission
and all the grandmothers
hold up the
sky
so all y'all can live
under it
and the new
king
said Oceans
were
the source of
his—and their
\ə-'grēv-mənt\ syndrome-
pathology-
affliction-
disorder-
condition

He strangles each audience
member—it takes 4 years—
and eats the dry ground
out from under
tiny philosophers
just for fun

The Great Jiu Jitsu Move of Being

Stand like a horse
on a street named
Your Grandmother's Best Friend Who
Made You Grilled Cheese
Used To Live Here Rd.

and with your back
to the sun
name just one person
who would die for you
or melt cheese for you

next realize

you should have spent a lifetime
learning to sing for her

or ringing the neck
of a trombone for her

or how to move like water
so she can float down you

—A. River

nothing roiling

just a ride for her

all her shitty memories vague
and quiet now

It's Raining Refrigerators

I don't need saving
She said

And yeah—
I know she
has the power
to put a spell on
at least one person

But I've got nothing else
planned for today

This Tinier Opus

I know this:

that typewriters
make you fall on your sword
in a foreign country

that a bow drawn
across the viola
founders a whaling ship

that next-door-clacking-
keystrokes
tilting with
letters
drawn like bingo
sweet steel-
silk-and-feather

make poetry

and that this
hardly sings

nor festoons a nothing
flowers a no one
forgets a nowhere
fandangos a never
dresses us up
in villainy
—calls it justice

¿and where-away
 the whales?

and
¿how is it
 we all make do
 with only two
 hands
 with all there is
 to slap and tickle?

on a swirl of road

I drop-a-day to pieces
and become a blur
trampling roses

the better people
have analogue clock faces
and are as true as a laugh
in any language

we all make do
on banana-peel-shoes
or stumble out
a word so shining
even the gods
marvel at our boomcrash

some descending true
to madness
on the last ship
floating

but that make for good reading

no naturally-crooked
thing
will be set straight

without a good war

she—

—stripping sheep-guts
to stitch for bagpipes
to burn the plains
for a king

we are all peering and tiny
with conversations
wriggling

a new conundrum
in every eardrum

I don't speak Catalan
or Occitan

I don't English well

Kaddish:
　never read it
God:
　never met 'em

Holy:
　never felt it
She:
　never knew
he
who (like me)

never laid bare

never was able to

pull it out of the
chest once lodged

Deep:
—never swam it

Sleep:
a fall
   a swirl
      a babe
swaddled in the souvenir of
Quiet memory:
     never heard it

now I can't tell television
    from television

I took the pizzicato for a chariot
in 2 easy steps:

1. With enough reverb
  on a plucked
  string
  you get an asylum

2. With enough
  dust and Dolby
  you get Ben Hur

anyway—
  of course
  There's always

A horse

never an end
till the olde men
filibuster
and throw funeral guts
floating-bloated on the Ganges

I'm not Dulcinea'd
atop no Rocinante
I am Sanchovoid
but
oh-skip-to-this end

a question
in the form of
a poem:
*¿what good
is a wasp?*

¿anyone?

everyone: dancing to distraction
everyone: drawing a bow
everyone: an Icarus
everyone: a Lazarus
everyone: mothdrawn
        to the piano keys
everyone: upside down
        holy-mother-wreck-of-eyes
        pretty
everyone: as meddlesome as a cleric
everyone: a door to some inside
everyone: breathing a room
everyone: a scoundrel
everyone: trombone-befuddled and
        wishing on the mermaid

everyone: slobbering
        pennycake-eaters
everyone: a chorus-ad-infinitum
        a couple
        a family
        a tribe
        a flag
        the bomb
everyone: backbreaking-inconceivable
everyone: dumbfounded-buddhamonsters

everyone: a broken-hearted
        heart-breaker
        smiling-up the volcano
        leaping-from-the-bridge-waving
everyone: a faction of
        one   in the end
        a hero of their own epic shit
everyone: dark
         and brooding
          and s t r a n g e
          as nighttime
everyone: a million-to-one shot and getting
        better with the moon—worse
        with the tide
everyone: star-staring-lonely
                    and away
no better beasts
to marvel at

   lovely meandering fools
   longsuffering
   godbeautiful

   breaching for air

Every Dog Has Its Day

She told me

and at first I thought
she meant me

because of this tiny bit
of good fortune I'd had
winning the Allen Gruber
poetry prize for substandard
equivalence

But then I thought no,
 can't be that

She must mean
actually every
actual dog
actually having an
actual day

like if a dog accidentally barked
the word deciduous

that—even if accidental,
would be a thing worth
celebrating with a special
day for him

or saving a little kid from
tumbling down the elevator shaft
of a burning building
during a flood

same—
and that dog would get her own day

a whole actual day of treats
and belly rubs by enthusiastic,
actual clowns
and cars to chase in a safe,
controlled environment

Wow, I said, smiling
off into the rising sun—
To be a dog! To inevitably
get your own day… Mmm!

She cleared her throat
and when I looked back
she had the

— Strangest—
expression on
her beautiful face

and I caught a glimpse
of recognition in her eyes

that we were thinking the
actual same thing

Or maybe it was possible
that in all this that is
the word

She was feeling that most
unpleasant of self-
inflicted maladies,

Envy

A Festival

Whoever
gathered
50 poets

together
in one
place
to read
100
Poems

in
some finite
time
doesn't
undress
like
the rest
of us

—they
set fire
to their
clothes

and sit
facing
West
politely
waiting
for
the sun to rise

The Sun Is Reluctant Today

a crossing guard holds up traffic
for a middle-aged dwarf with bad skin

the moon left some residue in the sky

the cost of gasoline is sneering

violins have taken over the radio
and refuse to negotiate

everywhere more plastic things
join the big plastic party

somewhere
a tree gives up
and learns to love the lathe
and become some bowl

a woman in bed is left wanting
while some fool streaks diesel smoke
over the horizon

traffic just won the award for
highest concentration of misery
created in a single hour

a sharpened no.2 pencil is sick of waiting
for direction

something vital for a breakfast
staged a coup with gravity

a murder of crows
refuses to render a verdict

pensive flags on poles waiting on the wind

a couple guys forget to shake on it
and some part of the universe
winced~

and on that corner

came unhinged

Politics

Here's a secret:

I keep Rachmaninoff
chained-up in my basement

your turn

Some Conclusions
Made While Living as
a Fading Ember:

Your hair is full of
late-19th century
greed
this is something
angular in you
to know about—
but—by any mid-century
standard
we're all submarines
bumping into each
other like wedding-
goers or a room
full of desperate
musicians
selling you their bad
music on a format
no one
loves anymore while
you're trying
to be a better
person
like a chair any-
one can sit on for free
and find the Bottom
of the World
quietly
It is a fire surrounding
a concrete hotel
in an East Germany
with no view
where a woman lives

like the Caretaker
in The Shining
—just her
without an axe
only a keyboard
—she caresses
the letters out of:
Intention
Intention
Intention
	the light cut holes
	in her cigarette smoke
—something turns
in the gut of the
now undone
confetti king
on his private hospice ship
the banjo-kazoo
orchestra fading
outside an increasingly
opaque porthole and
an ocean outside
fading to blank

3C 273

Here is the weltschmerz world / where no self-respecting kid thanks a crossing guard / and waves break over astronaut-dreams / and no fires worth talking about extinguishing before breakfast / where we humble before eggs / and especially bacon / it's Monday-feels-like-we're-all-gonna-die / yesterday meant my left-eye leaving or already left /a de-orbiting little Mir over a south Pacific sky / ¿and did we think to forge a thanks to the god of the ground against gravity / or amen to streets of wandering rags / and thankyou for offering-up some middling-hug with smiles / but what they really need is a good dog / and the means to stay alive so they can love the dog / now you're in the frame of a beautiful film / by a beautifully tragic director / who took his own life finally / his wife couldn't eat soup without getting it in her eyebrows and talked loudly about future trips to Italy / it was too late to clever-tongue his way away / and all his Khrushcheving of the kitchen table was only a tiny spectacle / and enough was enough and gravity was enormous / and the fall: a glorious never-ending pie fight / then comes the emperor of those pinwheel-wielding-fools-six-ways-to-Sunday / and it will be the surest sign to fall for love again / to relish with flourish and grand gestures / like divorce papers waved in the face of the accountant of bad relationships / and dreams / find 3C 273's conquering light / become ridiculous for just the existence of it / celestial and older than God or the house he was born in / i tell the tiny orbiting-eye to shut it / that if we stop and stare at our bare feet long enough / there's laughing till we see through to the truth / that we're all in some slow-motion Somme / some constant Cannae / which was just a large-scale military hug with milk-and-cookies-machine-guns and bloody sleep after / we're cataloging planets we've yet to discover / and like a Laika / on a ride of epic-anyways / and whoever doesn't contribute to interesting conversation / will be asked to get out of the Buick

/ blue / and on which the reflection of a planet no one can see otherwise / shines and shines and shines till laughter boredom and sighs / i think i'll thank the tollbooth workers before they're all gone—i miss them already / like i miss the crazy we left to die for lack of feeding / or that space-station / –it's like it was just here / like Russian fits of knuckles wrapped in cracker-packets of silver / we're all sick from lack of caring / it Sundays us again / and we're a mess / we killed a squirrel out of a tree / and when it dropped at our feet we declared it a beautiful animal / but our friend or lover or / mother or father sister or brother declared us / a beautiful shot

Most Sundays at the Roadside Scripture Repair Stand

This is superfluous
she said trimming
the letters T E L E
from the word *telephone*
and a god with
trembling hands
thumbed a Rolodex
for the number of
someone
who would agree
the word *Superfluous*
was a bit much in this context
—Meanwhile
I picked up a book
dangling next to this drama
titled Right Now
and read along as it unfolded

It's a Long Way to Go for Nothing

and no one owes anyone a listen

no one's owed a hand
or a little sip of joy

no one gets any insight
while God's in town

forget it—
and remember:

if the fish heads
come back to life
(and they will)
they'll go on and on
about this and that

and you'll be sorry
you didn't get on that train
when you had the chance

it's a long way to go for nothing

I'll hold your sorrow
in my left hand
my right is for me

and the stars
are drilled
in iron tonight

above us

Circe
Oil, Mid-Century
(from memory)

If the crimson
of her lips
would have his

he'd kiss the canvas

she'd mock him
for that hunger
he remembers

and twists
the line of her mouth
into a smirk

steps back

—starving

When Science Took Over
or
How to Believe a Queen
When She Says "I Love You"

He built a contraption
to trap a queen's thoughts
—a gimbaled thing
so he could examine them
upright—even on the rough
sea of his doubt—and in her
forlorn face and sleepstarved eyes
where even gravity didn't
stand a chance
he died
over and over
A king believes no one—
He thought—but
A good king will spend
a lifetime believing a queen
who asked only the kingdom
of his body to rest on
and sleep

Boxing for Flowers

Somewhere in the future
the last television
will shine to life and
clad in shimmering sarcasm
the last pugilist
in the world
will punch the last lazy clown
for the sake of Debussy
or Kandinsky then crumple
crying in static to a flurry of piano keys
and someone will say
the boxer did it for us
for US
the good life is what we got—
metaphor
delivered
metaphorically
—that
and a black eye

Regret

¿that poem you wrote and said
if I ever tell anyone about
I'll kill you?
I will submit it to a prestigious place
—it will be accepted
I'll get book deals from it
I'll win a writing-grant
that is vaguely more
than the one you got
I will live happily-ever-after
—my Aristotelian-bent—
¿and you?
    softly
       nightly
          you'll weep-yourself to something
                        like
                          sleep
thinking of when you abandoned a good poem
into the hands of an idiot

Dulcinea
in Paint-Splattered Shoes

Some god or other paints
as Turner—
the one: "Fishermen at Sea"
but there are no fishermen
and no sea
just the insanity of love's
driven-wild-slowmoving
sandstorm of a sky
and they without flying camels

Undone by their
No's
and
We've got to go's
their train huffing
at the station
his sea a dumb rage
and the fishermen
somewhere fucked
under a Turner sky

No One Ever Died

at the plastic banana factory
—It's true
you can check it—
and no one ever will
but someday someone will
(die)
at the Large Hadron Collider
probably from a stray subatomic particle
or a broken heart

¿OVER HOW?

(erasure from a long-forgotten document)

de text zat is rad
comes a surprise –
de rust ate open even the bee
cut n ran the anonymous ark
rend a thrill
ring a number unknown
sex a part
but bound to what these ripped ages ply
–played ragged maps to no place
head –bored –show mine eyes
parting an ideal world is true
–the act all nag and worry
someone does a lie-hide-and press
–I taught age
so I spin and demand a think
see her (and definite law –perhaps)
   that decade met me to pieces
Ich "es ass"
that other ample cult ate
the contemporary world
  is above
   is pen
    is our vile hat
–ire ate his words
I left in d gust
singly filled red with style
into ultimate happy rhythms
and punk friends
to sorrow for
are judged all the same
the in-judges differ in taste
and dislikes

out out —out his torture
worlds for words —vision
is distraction-enough to lock her numb
the climb —inter-able-ism —an empty fix
I rode an India like fire
an India smiling and put in your pocket
come fly soup and warm
you think exact —lie —change places
hide-out inside white Miami
sun and smile but it cracks
so you aint pleasant
it's on ¿see? —good

My Fake Door Is Sadder Than
All the Fake Doors There Ever Were

Like how we all die into an ocean
and only once

While a slow-moving postal truck loaded
with counterfeit Mona Lisas

Breaks our efforts at avoiding endings
and never stops to deliver anything

We stupid all over the place
like rudderless fire trucks

Halting against an invisible leash of feeling and
backward-over-the-shoulder little

Kid-glances we'll have to wait till old age
to mourn properly

It gets worse—and for extra sadness
imagine all the outside

Is a home surrounded by fire
with all the world's parents inside

Kingdom of Plates and Bowls Filled and Waiting

There must be a place
in the world
where dessert after breakfast
is a thing
there is where I'll set up my kingdom
it will always be dawn there
every good citizen will be
a weak-chinned sleepyhead
there will be awards for the best of them
and the awards will be presented with
humility by genuine tough guys who
openly read books in bars and
who won't receive rewards
partly because
they wouldn't accept them
anyway

Plowed-Under-Sleeping-Empire-Ladies

from over here
—from (say)
America where
everywhere else is
Carthage

a piano might remind us
to be in a movie about despair

and old ladies laughing
sounds like crying

the desert is no place to
mourn
the Arctic is no place to
mourn

you need timid little animals
to mourn properly

they come up to you
you pat them
you're done

Inscription It'd Be Cool to See on a Headstone

the ships are all burned

there's no turning back

when you're a beast of a thing

like me

a fiction of eyes pulling me down

all I want is to stay in this tree

draw me in lemon juice

write me up
        lower case

I sit on the moon

in a can

the bringer of dry lakebed

wrapped in a nightmare

a dim dumb brute is I am

Epilogue

—and then the crew
for the sake of the voyage
and the sanctity of the sun
groped their way
for the love of the poem
to a New Captain
offering the balls of the
olde one to the new
as an un-refusable meal
in celebration of
sinking ships piloted
by ascendant novices
everywhere and fantastic
and livid with dancing
on decks saturated
with the blood of the 1st mate

The Anarcho-Cinnamon-Swirl-Ravioli-Death-Squad
Vs.
The Old Admiral

The trees!
the old admiral argued
to the sky head-cracked

the pavement as cold
as unyielding epistemology
while ambulances slid
dreamily
from curb
to curb like
baying for warmer weather

like mother's milk
and missing him
over and over

now as heavy-water
creeping up on a drain
an accumulated mess of nows
a dull throb of effectiveness
like a slow-motion waiter
serving a plated-omelet to the ministry of
the hungry-heavy-bored

from here Paris is a cleaver
held between breaths with accents
an annoyance to something
unreachable in him
the world-clearly peopled
by the mustachio'd and sickle-fingered

fetid-now
rank-dejected the old admiral sank

1st do no harm

his accent *was* all hand-waving and dancing in place
his hair was once revolutionary
and the sun did hide
from him
refusing to grant the cast of a shadow

and even the most dogged of the dogs were only
loaves of bread on sticks before him
and the leaves took leave of the trees
rather than admit their less-than fanciful-ness

and all the trifling domestics with
white-leather interiors were his to parade
and his razor's-edge trousers
licked the bright of his shoes

his politics were
IMPECCABLE

and his mom is
all punctuation
a book of griefs
mixing bowls
and missing scissors

hers was repose in response
to all the little admiral's drownings

and just behind the teeth

where the tongue
grates and curls

a serpent for the argument

strangely she ended
with Johnny Cash on her lips

then at last awash in a sea of
puny arguments
playthings winged
with all that happiness missing
and a favorite in his sister's
Sulking Competition

and after all that tumbling
through time coming to rest at rank
but never putting to use those
chic-chick spies

but brain-storming about
the best in-scale explosions or what-in-blazes
are 1800 thread-count Egyptian sheets...

now from his odd horizontal he eyes
the ever-ancient-new beatniks
sporting the best in Chinese-wisdom-beards
walking cats on leashes
mutterings like underwater violins
with underbreath saxophones in cellars
to confuse him more
he reaches back
for those strange and doubtful buckaroos
he knew—now gone

now the sliver is off the bone
the red is off the brick
and the thumbs are up
sniffing at the cosmos

the old admiral is cooking

for the 1st time the old admiral is amused

then ever and only unfolded otherwise
in books
infernal machines
to make the best
in capitalist
ice creams he thinks:

If immortal me
all immortal be —and *so you're welcome*

in dreams

where—away-and-aloft
the old admiral's *uncle*
long ago gone on gasoline heels
chasing an angel in an el-dorado
to the tune of *I'm An Animal*
and so there went that hero

and awake

he amassed truths upon truths like;

no one shies-away from December

and that;

for all his tough-guy talk
Burroughs had only ever shot his own
wife

and *thus art*
the admiral conceded
as he kept knee deep
at her grave

then more and more
his diminishing bewilderment at
shit-kicking Baptists
flags
and fornicating horses on parade

now thrown from all the thrills
a revelation a shrug:

no one *wins in January*
and now February is coming no matter what

the old admiral's observations while afloat

if from Toronto
you drive like this

(when finally foundered)

tiny little jockeys race tiny little horses
round tiny little churches

meanwhile his want:

in his utopia—
a kingdom of waiting patiently and forever
all complaint banished on pain of boredom
not a single tricycle is thrown in anger
and all the little girls would never know
a Nabokov

the old admiral
a maximum ogre
tied trilling to a tree
and taunted

always all he could ever muster
was the smallest talk
pseudo-stern and wandering
like eating prideful with a flimsy fork
employees must always *"ha"* he punched

and if he was the boss
he'll pulverize us all to a gas
and inhale us

¿bad?—yes
but inexplicably
he tipped well

a benevolent monster eye
falling-away finally with missiles still siloed—
in a mirror of ice and wandering sirens

and into the cold
a rodeo of baristas came
to poison him with cringes
and all the kids make neverminds of him

meaningless as an olde admiral

outside—from his fading—frozen horizontal and with
Chef Boyardee's ravioli death squad advancing
his mother in the fog of before
thumbing her catalog
of disappointments

in the Anarcho-Cinnamon-Swirl of memory
he sinks strangely with songs
of goats in his ears
into the bosom of Henry Kissinger

and sleeps-dreaming of the
time he defeated a whole country

took a wife

left her in Japan

On Opening the Last Page

Great and Slow Motion Acknowledgement is Made
to the Following:

Sad and lost car keys

Fiddly pieces of larger things waiting for glue

Anyone thought of as a "one man potato famine"

Any crow

Empty beaches filled with way too much horizon

Trying for optimism in a city filled with Russian composers
and museums full of art that has "something to say"

I've never done anything the gods of spring would approve of

What about you?

Acknowledgments

Thanks to the editors of the following publications, wherein some of these poems appeared: *The Arts Fuse, Bird's Thumb, Factory Hollow Press, Gambler Mag, Iterant, Jubilat, Lily Poetry Review, The Wilderness House Review* and *Wrestling with Poetry.*

Some of the poems in this collection first appeared in *It's Not Love Till Someone Loses an Eye,* published by Nixes Mate Press.

Special thanks to Eileen Cleary, a generous editor who took a chance on a big, strange book. Remember Eileen, regret can lead to personal growth...

Lastly, I would like to express my deepest appreciation to the big committee of humankind—you're all nuts. Thanks for that.

—C.
  '25

Clay Ventre lives and writes in New England.